This book is dedicated to my mother and father.

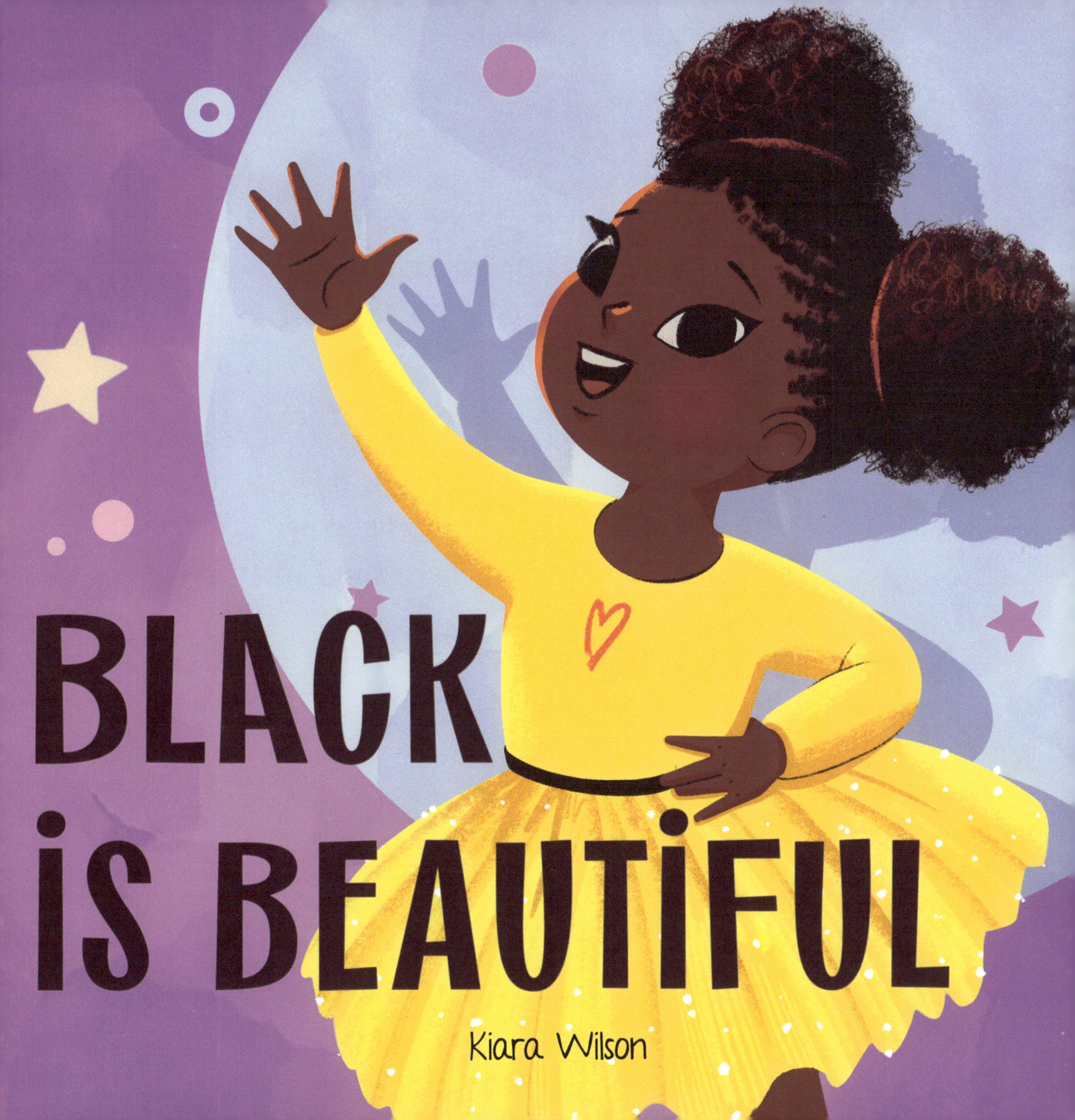

BLACK IS BEAUTIFUL

Kiara Wilson

When I look in the mirror,
I feel proud of what I see.
I am the only person
Who looks exactly like me.

I have big brown eyes,
And glistening brown black skin.
But it has taken me some time
To feel comfortable in the body I'm in.

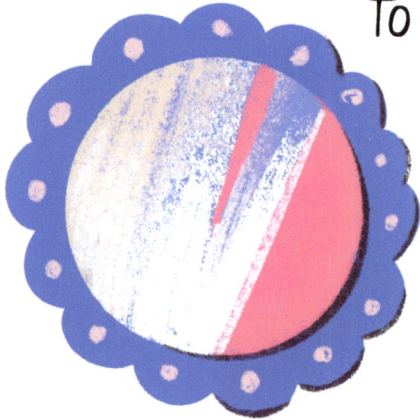

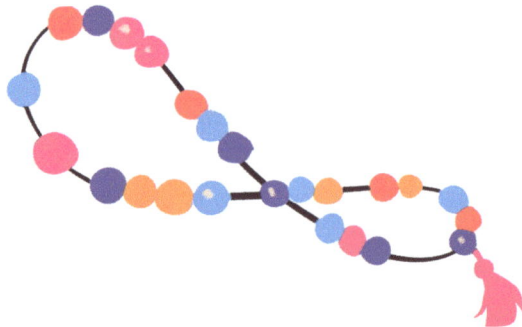

It took a while to realize
We are more than how we appear.
Being comfortable with my skin
Took me several years.

But now that I have,
I feel wonderful and free!
I've learned that black is beautiful
And I'm so happy to be me.

When I was little I wondered what it would be like,
To look like other girls...
To have bright blue eyes,
Soft and bouncy curls.

All the dolls at the store
Had white skin and blonde hair.
I'd try to look for toys like me,
But they were never there.

The princesses in storybooks
All look a certain way.
"They never look how I do,"
I'd look up to my mother and say.

At school, I would notice the same.
Few other kids looked how I look.
To see other black people,
I'd have to find them in history books.

I love playing on the playground,
At school or at the park.
When other kids make fun of me,
I'd feel like a target with a mark.

My hair is more coarse and bushy,
It's hardly ever smooth.
I usually wear it in a bun,
On top of my head in an up-do.

Because my skin is darker,
I've felt alone sometimes.
Feeling different and unusual
Has made me want to hide.

But my mother pointed out,
I am perfect and beautiful this way.
My skin color makes me unique,
I can proudly say.

I've learned I'm not alone.
The world is full of different colors,
For if we all looked the same,
Life would be so much duller.

When I'm in a room full of people,
My skin tone does stand out,
But it's only one of my features
People notice as I walk about.

I like to wear bright colors.
They look great against my skin.
When I'm not feeling pretty on the outside,
I remember that what's important is within.

I am kind to all people,
Regardless of their race.
I see people for who they are,
And look beyond the color of their face.

Being black is beautiful,
I'm comfortable in my skin.
I proudly wear my heritage,
And where my ancestors have been.

I learn about my culture.
I'm so proud of my family.
Because of their strength and sacrifices,
I am able to be here and free.

I am confident in my color.
I feel pretty when I see my face.
I no longer walk in a room,
And feel out of place.

I don't need anyone's approval,
To feel the way I do.
I am confident in who I am,
And I wish the same for you!